Berberine

A Beginner's Guide to Balancing Blood Sugar, Managing Weight, and a 5-Step Plan to Get Started

copyright © 2025 Stephanie Hinderock

All rights reserved No part of this book may be reproduced, or stored in a retrieval system, or transmitted in any form or by any means, electronic, mechanical, photocopying, recording, or otherwise, without express written permission of the publisher.

Disclaimer

By reading this disclaimer, you are accepting the terms of the disclaimer in full. If you disagree with this disclaimer, please do not read the guide.

All of the content within this guide is provided for informational and educational purposes only, and should not be accepted as independent medical or other professional advice. The author is not a doctor, physician, nurse, mental health provider, or registered nutritionist/dietician. Therefore, using and reading this guide does not establish any form of a physician-patient relationship.

Always consult with a physician or another qualified health provider with any issues or questions you might have regarding any sort of medical condition. Do not ever disregard any qualified professional medical advice or delay seeking that advice because of anything you have read in this guide. The information in this guide is not intended to be any sort of medical advice and should not be used in lieu of any medical advice by a licensed and qualified medical professional.

The information in this guide has been compiled from a variety of known sources. However, the author cannot attest to or guarantee the accuracy of each source and thus should not be held liable for any errors or omissions.

You acknowledge that the publisher of this guide will not be held liable for any loss or damage of any kind incurred as a result of this guide or the reliance on any information provided within this guide. You acknowledge and agree that you assume all risk and responsibility for any action you undertake in response to the information in this guide.

Using this guide does not guarantee any particular result (e.g., weight loss or a cure). By reading this guide, you acknowledge that there are no guarantees to any specific outcome or results you can expect.

All product names, diet plans, or names used in this guide are for identification purposes only and are the property of their respective owners. The use of these names does not imply endorsement. All other trademarks cited herein are the property of their respective owners.

Where applicable, this guide is not intended to be a substitute for the original work of this diet plan and is, at most, a supplement to the original work for this diet plan and never a direct substitute. This guide is a personal expression of the facts of that diet plan.

Where applicable, persons shown in the cover images are stock photography models and the publisher has obtained the rights to use the images through license agreements with third-party stock image companies.

Table of Contents

Introduction   7
What Is Berberine?   9
   Understanding This Natural Compound   10
   History and Traditional Uses   11
   Why It's Gaining Popularity Today   12
How Berberine Works in the Body   14
   Activating AMPK: The Metabolic Master Switch   14
   Effects on Blood Sugar Regulation   15
   Impact on Cholesterol and Fat Metabolism   16
Proven Health Benefits of Berberine   18
   Managing Blood Sugar and Type 2 Diabetes   18
   Supporting Weight Loss and Fat Metabolism   19
   Improving Heart Health   20
   Enhancing Gut Health and Combating Infections   21
   Hormonal Balance and PCOS Support   22
Choosing the Right Berberine Supplement   24
   What to Look for on the Label   24
   Forms of Berberine (HCl, Berberine Complexes)   26
   Quality and Dosage Guidelines   27
5-Step Plan to Get Started with Berberine Supplementation   30
   Step 1: Identify Your Health Goals   30
   Step 2: Start with the Right Dosage   35
   Step 3: Pair Berberine with Diet and Lifestyle Changes   40
   Step 4: Monitor Your Progress   44
   Step 5: Adjust Your Routine for Long-Term Benefits   50
Enhancing Results with Lifestyle Changes   57
   Dietary Tips for Blood Sugar and Weight Management   57
   Exercise Recommendations to Boost Metabolism   60
   Stress Management and Sleep Optimization   62

Potential Side Effects and How to Handle Them	**65**
Digestive Upset	65
Lowered Blood Sugar	66
Allergic Reactions	67
Practical Tips for Managing Mild Side Effects	68
When to Consult a Doctor	69
Monitoring Your Health	70
Avoiding Pitfalls and Maximizing Benefits	**72**
Timing and Frequency of Doses	72
Interactions with Medications	74
Practical Advice for Avoiding Pitfalls	76
Conclusion	**80**
FAQs	**83**
References and Helpful Links	**86**

Introduction

Berberine has been making waves in the world of health and wellness — and for good reason. This natural compound, derived from plants like barberry and goldenseal, comes with a fascinating history that dates back centuries. Traditionally used in ancient medicine, Berberine is now gaining recognition for its potential to promote better health in a variety of ways. From supporting blood sugar regulation to improving heart health and even helping with hormonal imbalances, this natural remedy has a lot to offer. However, as with any supplement, stepping into this territory requires caution and the guidance of a healthcare professional.

You might have heard Berberine touted as a game-changer for managing blood sugar levels. This is because it activates AMPKa — often called a "metabolic master switch" — which plays a key role in glucose and fat metabolism. But its benefits don't stop there. Berberine has been studied for its potential to aid weight loss, lower cholesterol, and improve gut health by balancing the microbiome. It may even provide support for those dealing with PCOS, offering a natural way to promote hormonal balance.

While this all sounds promising, it's important to remember that no supplement is a one-size-fits-all solution. If you're intrigued by Berberine, your first step should always be consulting your physician to determine whether it's a safe and appropriate choice for you.

In this guide, we will talk about the following;

- What is Berberine?
- How Berberine Works in the Body
- Proven Health Benefits of Berberine
- Choosing the Right Berberine Supplement
- 5-Step Plan to Get Started with Berberine
- Enhancing Results with Lifestyle Changes
- Potential Side Effects and How to Handle Them
- Avoiding Pitfalls and Maximizing Benefits

By the time you finish this guide, you'll have a deeper understanding of Berberine — what it is, how it works, and how it fits into the bigger picture of health and wellness. Whether you're just curious or seriously considering Berberine as part of your routine, this resource gives you the tools to take the next step with confidence and clarity. Just remember, better health starts with informed choices, and your doctor should always be part of that conversation.

What Is Berberine?

Berberine is a bioactive compound with deep roots in the natural world. Chemically, Berberine belongs to a group of naturally occurring compounds known as alkaloids, which are characterized by their nitrogen-based structures and notable physiological effects on living organisms. Its chemical structure forms a bright yellow pigment, one of its most recognizable traits, and has historically been used as a natural dye.

This compound is primarily sourced from specific plants, including barberry (Berberis vulgaris), goldenseal (Hydrastis canadensis), and Oregon grape (Mahonia aquifolium). These plants store Berberine within their roots, stems, bark, and occasionally their rhizomes.

As a natural compound, Berberine stands out for its versatility and accessibility. Simple yet powerful, it transcends cultures and continents in its applications, proof of its enduring relevance in both ancient and modern healthcare. Despite being a historical remedy, Berberine is far more than a relic of traditional practices—it's a scientifically intriguing molecule that continues to captivate researchers and wellness enthusiasts alike.

Understanding This Natural Compound

Scientifically speaking, Berberine is a powerhouse. Much of its activity stems from its interaction with adenosine monophosphate-activated protein kinase (AMPK), an enzyme often referred to as the "metabolic master switch." AMPK plays a central role in regulating how your body handles energy production and storage. When Berberine activates AMPK, it initiates a cascade of processes that can improve energy balance, promote healthy metabolism, and regulate blood sugar. This makes it especially promising for those managing metabolic disorders, such as Type 2 diabetes.

However, Berberine's benefits don't stop with AMPK activation. Its influence extends to the gut microbiome, the ecosystem of bacteria living in your digestive system. Research suggests that Berberine helps foster a healthier balance among these microbes, potentially reducing harmful bacteria and encouraging beneficial strains. This interaction may explain some of its effects on digestion, inflammatory conditions, and even immunity.

Lastly, Berberine has shown promise in affecting lipid metabolism, which involves how the body processes fats. Studies suggest Berberine can lower cholesterol and triglyceride levels, making it a candidate for managing heart health. This combination of effects—on metabolism, gut health, and lipid levels—positions Berberine as a uniquely multifaceted compound.

History and Traditional Uses

The history of Berberine stretches back thousands of years, with its use recorded in several ancient medicinal systems. Traditional Chinese Medicine (TCM) utilizes Berberine for its antimicrobial and anti-inflammatory properties. Practitioners commonly prescribed it for issues like diarrhea, gastrointestinal infections, and bacterial conditions. Its bright yellow extract earned it a place not only as a remedy but also as a dye used in ancient Chinese textiles.

Meanwhile, Ayurveda, the traditional healing system of India, also found value in Berberine-rich plants. Remedies featuring Berberine were used to address skin conditions, digestive ailments, and wound infections. Its antibacterial qualities made it an indispensable natural tool long before the development of modern antibiotics. Indigenous populations in North America also recognized the benefits of Berberine. Native American communities leveraged the medicinal properties of plants like barberry to treat infections and diarrhea, much like their Asian counterparts.

Berberine's long-standing reputation as a herbal healer is a testament to its efficacy and the intimate relationship between humans and nature over centuries.

Why It's Gaining Popularity Today

While Berberine has a storied past, its popularity in modern health circles is relatively recent. This resurgence can be attributed to increasing scientific studies that explore and validate its potential health benefits.

From regulating blood sugar levels to its role in heart health, Berberine is now seen as a promising agent for addressing chronic health issues that are prevalent today. For example, research into its effects on AMPK and metabolic function has highlighted its potential for managing Type 2 diabetes and supporting weight loss.

Modern wellness trends have also contributed to Berberine's reemergence. A growing demand for natural, plant-based remedies has propelled Berberine into the spotlight, particularly among those seeking alternatives to conventional medications. It's relatively easy to access in the form of capsules, powders, and tinctures, making it both convenient and appealing.

Beyond its physical benefits, Berberine's clean, plant-based origin aligns with the broader movement toward sustainability and earth-friendly health practices. People today are far more focused on holistic wellness—managing body, mind, and lifestyle in harmony—which dovetails perfectly with Berberine's multifaceted benefits.

Still, while Berberine's potential is exciting, it's important to proceed with care. It's not a miracle solution, and personal health contexts can vary widely. Consulting a physician remains essential before incorporating Berberine into your routine. Whether it's historical use or modern science piques your curiosity, Berberine's legacy and versatility make it a compelling subject, one that deserves a deeper look.

How Berberine Works in the Body

Berberine is a natural compound found in plants like barberry, goldenseal, and tree turmeric. Known for its vivid yellow color and long use in traditional medicine, berberine has recently gained attention for its potential health benefits. Among its many effects on the body, its ability to activate AMPK, regulate blood sugar, and improve cholesterol and fat metabolism stands out. Here's how it works.

Activating AMPK: The Metabolic Master Switch

One of berberine's core effects is its ability to activate an enzyme called AMPK (adenosine monophosphate-activated protein kinase). AMPK is often referred to as the "metabolic master switch" because it plays a key role in regulating energy balance within the body. When activated, AMPK promotes processes that generate energy while shutting down those that consume excess energy.

Berberine activates AMPK by reducing cellular energy levels (lowering ATP levels), which triggers the body to switch on AMPK to restore balance. Once AMPK is activated, it helps improve metabolic efficiency. This leads to benefits such as better glucose management, increased fat burning, and reduced storage of excess fats. Simply put, berberine flips the "on switch" for your body's energy regulation system, supporting a healthier metabolism.

Effects on Blood Sugar Regulation

One of the most impressive benefits of berberine is its effect on blood sugar regulation, which makes it a popular choice for people managing conditions like type 2 diabetes or prediabetes. By activating AMPK, berberine improves insulin sensitivity—how your body responds to insulin and uses it to lower blood sugar levels.

Berberine helps lower blood sugar through several mechanisms:

- *Improving glucose uptake:* Cells become more efficient at absorbing glucose from the bloodstream, reducing overall sugar levels.
- *Reducing glucose production in the liver:* The liver typically produces sugar (glucose) to maintain blood sugar stability. However, in people with diabetes, this production can go into overdrive. Berberine slows down this process, preventing spikes in blood sugar.
- *Slowing carbohydrate breakdown:* Berberine has been shown to reduce the activity of enzymes involved in

digesting carbohydrates, leading to slower absorption of sugar into the bloodstream after meals.

These combined actions help maintain steady blood sugar levels and reduce the fluctuations often associated with energy crashes or worsening insulin resistance.

Impact on Cholesterol and Fat Metabolism

Berberine's activation of AMPK also plays a crucial role in lipid metabolism—the way your body processes cholesterol and fats. By influencing these pathways, berberine can improve cholesterol levels and promote healthier fat storage and usage.

Effects on Cholesterol

Berberine has been shown to lower "bad" LDL cholesterol while increasing "good" HDL cholesterol. It achieves this by:

- **Boosting LDL clearance:** Berberine increases the number of LDL receptors on liver cells, prompting the liver to remove more LDL cholesterol from the bloodstream.
- **Reducing cholesterol production:** It inhibits a key enzyme involved in making cholesterol (similar to how statin drugs work but with a more natural mechanism).

Effects on Fat Metabolism

Additionally, berberine supports fat metabolism by encouraging fat burning and decreasing fat storage. By activating AMPK, berberine signals the body to use stored fat as a source of energy, which may contribute to weight management. It can also reduce levels of triglycerides, another type of fat in the blood linked to heart health.

Berberine's effects on AMPK make it a powerful ally for those looking to improve their metabolic health. By activating this critical enzyme, berberine helps regulate blood sugar, improve insulin sensitivity, and support healthy cholesterol and fat metabolism.

Whether you're aiming to manage diabetes, support heart health, or maintain a balanced weight, berberine taps into your body's natural ability to maintain energy and metabolic balance. If you're considering adding berberine to your regimen, it's always a good idea to consult your healthcare provider to ensure it's right for you.

Proven Health Benefits of Berberine

Berberine, a natural compound found in plants like barberry, goldenseal, and tree turmeric, has been valued in traditional medicine for centuries. Modern research has uncovered a wide range of health benefits tied to this golden-yellow alkaloid, making it a sought-after natural remedy. From managing blood sugar to supporting heart and gut health, berberine addresses many common health concerns. Here's an in-depth look at the proven benefits:

Managing Blood Sugar and Type 2 Diabetes

One of the most well-documented benefits of berberine is its ability to regulate blood sugar levels, particularly for people with type 2 diabetes or prediabetes. It works through several mechanisms:

- *Improves insulin sensitivity:* Berberine enhances how your cells respond to insulin, reducing insulin resistance and allowing your body to use sugar more effectively.

- ***Reduces glucose production in the liver:*** It inhibits liver overproduction of glucose, which is a key factor in high blood sugar levels.
- ***Promotes glucose uptake in cells:*** Berberine helps move sugar out of the bloodstream and into your cells, where it can be used for energy.

Clinical studies have shown that berberine can lower fasting blood sugar levels and HbA1c (a long-term measure of blood sugar) as effectively as some prescription medications, including metformin. It can also help reduce spikes in blood sugar after meals, making it a powerful tool for blood sugar control.

Practical Tip:

If you're managing blood sugar, you can use berberine as a daily supplement alongside a healthy, balanced diet. Be sure to consult with a healthcare provider before adding it to your routine.

Supporting Weight Loss and Fat Metabolism

Berberine supports weight loss and helps regulate fat metabolism, making it a natural choice for those looking to shed extra pounds or improve their metabolic health.

- ***Activates AMPK:*** By activating AMPK, berberine boosts your body's metabolic efficiency and increases fat burning.

- ***Supports fat breakdown:*** It encourages the body to use stored fat for energy instead of storing it.
- ***Reduces fat buildup in the liver:*** Berberine can help prevent fatty liver disease, a condition linked to obesity and diabetes.

Studies have found that berberine supplementation may lead to modest weight loss and a decrease in BMI (body mass index). Additionally, it has been noted to lower levels of harmful triglycerides in the blood, contributing to better overall fat metabolism.

Practical Tip:

Combine berberine with regular exercise and a nutrient-rich diet to maximize its weight management effects.

Improving Heart Health

Berberine has several cardio-protective effects that support a healthy heart and circulatory system.

- ***Lowers LDL cholesterol:*** By increasing liver clearance of LDL ("bad") cholesterol, berberine helps reduce the risk of cardiovascular issues.
- ***Raises HDL cholesterol:*** It encourages higher levels of HDL ("good") cholesterol, which protects against artery blockages.

- *Lowers triglycerides:* High levels of triglycerides can increase your risk of heart disease, and berberine helps keep them in check.
- *Improves blood pressure:* Berberine can relax blood vessels, improve circulation, and reduce high blood pressure.

Studies suggest that berberine's effects on lipids are comparable to those of some prescription cholesterol-lowering drugs but with fewer side effects. This makes it a natural and effective option to support heart health.

Practical Tip:

If you have high cholesterol or other heart concerns, berberine can complement lifestyle changes like healthy eating, exercise, and stress management.

Enhancing Gut Health and Combating Infections

Berberine also benefits the gut microbiome and has antimicrobial properties, making it effective against bacterial, fungal, and parasitic infections.

- *Balances gut bacteria:* Berberine supports healthy gut bacteria by reducing harmful strains. It has shown promise in managing conditions such as Small Intestinal Bacterial Overgrowth (SIBO) and irritable bowel syndrome (IBS).

- *Fights infections:* Its antimicrobial effects help combat infections like H. pylori (which can cause stomach ulcers) and Candida overgrowth.
- *Reduces inflammation in the gut:* Berberine has anti-inflammatory effects that soothe the digestive tract, benefiting conditions like colitis.

By tackling both microbial imbalances and inflammation, berberine helps improve digestion and overall gut health.

Practical Tip:

If you're dealing with gut or digestive issues, consider berberine as part of a broader strategy that includes probiotics and a gut-friendly diet.

Hormonal Balance and PCOS Support

Berberine shows promise for women with polycystic ovary syndrome (PCOS), a condition commonly associated with insulin resistance, irregular periods, and hormone imbalances.

- *Improves insulin resistance:* Since PCOS is often linked to insulin resistance, berberine's blood sugar-regulating benefits can have a direct positive impact on symptoms.
- *Regulates androgens:* By improving insulin sensitivity, berberine helps reduce androgen levels, which are often elevated in women with PCOS. Lower

androgen levels can improve symptoms like acne and irregular cycles.
- ***Supports weight management:*** Many women with PCOS struggle with weight gain, and berberine's role in enhancing fat metabolism can assist in achieving a healthier weight.

Several studies suggest that berberine may be as effective as common medications used to manage PCOS but with fewer side effects.

Practical Tip:

For women with PCOS, combining berberine with healthy lifestyle habits and a low-glycemic diet may lead to noticeable improvements in symptoms.

Berberine is a powerful natural compound with a broad range of health benefits. From managing blood sugar and supporting weight loss to improving heart health and balancing hormones, its versatility and effectiveness are backed by scientific research.

Whether you're looking to address a specific health concern or simply enhance overall wellness, berberine might be a worthy addition to your routine. Always check with your healthcare provider before starting any new supplement to ensure it's a good fit for your needs.

Choosing the Right Berberine Supplement

When considering integrating Berberine into your wellness routine, choosing the right supplement is key to achieving effective results. With a variety of forms, brands, and dosages available, navigating the supplement aisle can be overwhelming. This chapter will guide you through the essential factors to consider when selecting a Berberine supplement, ensuring you make an informed and reliable choice.

What to Look for on the Label

The first step in selecting a quality Berberine supplement is understanding how to read the label. Here's what to prioritize:

1. ***Concentration of Berberine:*** Look for supplements that specify the concentration of active Berberine per serving. A standard dose of Berberine is typically 500 mg, taken two to three times daily. Avoid products that fail to clearly indicate the amount of Berberine

included, as this could point to ineffective or diluted formulations.
2. *Additional Ingredients:* Some Berberine supplements include complementary ingredients designed to enhance absorption or provide additional health benefits. For example, milk thistle or black pepper extract (piperine) is sometimes added to improve bioavailability. While additional ingredients can be beneficial, ensure they are listed clearly and are well-researched for safety and effectiveness.
3. *Certifications and Testing:* Opt for supplements that carry certifications like Good Manufacturing Practices (GMP) or NSF International certification, which indicate compliance with high-quality production standards. Third-party testing by independent labs is another critical marker of quality and purity, as it ensures the product contains what it claims and lacks harmful contaminants.
4. *Free From Fillers:* Avoid supplements with unnecessary fillers, artificial colors, or additives. A clean label with minimal binders or excipients is generally a sign of a higher-quality product.
5. *Allergen Information:* If you have allergies or specific dietary restrictions, check the label for potential allergens like gluten, soy, or lactose. Many high-quality supplements will specify whether they are

free from common allergens and are vegan or non-GMO certified.

When choosing a Berberine supplement, look for transparency in labeling, reputable certifications and testing, and minimal fillers or allergens. As always, consult with your healthcare provider before adding any new supplement to your routine.

Forms of Berberine (HCl, Berberine Complexes)

Berberine supplements come in various forms, and understanding these differences can help you choose the one best suited for your needs.

1. **Berberine HCl:**

    This is the most common and widely used form of Berberine, known for its high stability and effectiveness. Berberine HCl (hydrochloride) is typically well-absorbed and offers standardized potency. It's an excellent option for general metabolic and cardiovascular support.

2. **Berberine Complexes:**

    Some supplements use Berberine combined with other compounds to accelerate absorption or improve its activity in the body. For instance, Berberine bound with phospholipids or other bio-enhancers is considered to have better bioavailability.

One such example is "Berberine phytosome," which is a complex designed to enhance absorption compared to standard Berberine HCl. If you struggle with digesting other supplements or are looking for enhanced efficiency, these complexes might be beneficial.

Regardless of the form, the therapeutic benefits of Berberine rely heavily on its correct dosage and consistent usage rather than the form alone.

Quality and Dosage Guidelines

Choosing a high-quality supplement involves more than just reading the label – you need to dig into the source and manufacturing processes.

1. **Purity and Sourcing**

    Investigate the source of the Berberine. Top-tier supplements use Berberine extracted from plants like Berberis aristata. Be cautious of products from unknown manufacturers or those that don't disclose sourcing information, as lower-quality products may contain contaminants or be less potent.

2. **Manufacturing Practices**

   Look for products from reputable brands that use GMP-certified facilities. This guarantees that the supplement meets strict regulations for safety and consistency. Research the manufacturer's reputation and read reviews to verify credibility.

3. **Dosage Recommendations**

   The dosage of Berberine is crucial for effective results. Research indicates that a dose of 500 mg, taken two to three times daily with meals, is optimal for supporting blood sugar regulation and metabolic health. This schedule ensures a steady concentration of the compound in your system throughout the day.

4. **Start with Lower Doses**

   For first-time users, starting with a lower dose (e.g., 300 mg) and gradually increasing to the recommended 500 mg can minimize potential side effects such as digestive discomfort.

5. **Consistency Over Time**

   Berberine works best when taken consistently over several weeks to months. Incorporating it into a routine alongside regular meals helps enhance absorption and ensures long-term compliance.

6. **Consult a Healthcare Provider**

   Always consult your doctor before starting Berberine, particularly if you take other medications or have underlying health conditions. Dosages may need to be adjusted based on your unique health profile.

Choosing the right Berberine supplement requires attention to factors like potency, form, manufacturing quality, and proper dosage. By understanding what to look for on the label, the differences between Berberine HCl and complexes, and the importance of sourcing and testing, you can ensure you're investing in a supplement that delivers real results without unnecessary risks. Ultimately, pairing a high-quality product with informed usage will maximize Berberine's potential benefits for your health.

5-Step Plan to Get Started with Berberine Supplementation

Berberine supplements can offer numerous health benefits, from improving blood sugar control to aiding weight loss and heart health. Getting started with berberine supplementation is simple when you follow a structured plan. Below is a 5-step guide to help you begin your berberine journey effectively and safely.

Step 1: Identify Your Health Goals

Before you begin taking berberine, it's essential to understand why you're using it and what you aim to achieve. Having a clear purpose not only keeps you motivated but also helps you measure its effectiveness over time. Here's how to identify your health goals and lay the foundation for success:

1. **Define Your Specific Goals**

    Start by asking yourself what you hope to accomplish with berberine. Your health goals may vary depending on your unique needs. Here are some common objectives people have when using berberine:

- ***Blood Sugar Management:*** If you're looking to balance blood sugar levels, berberine might help by improving insulin sensitivity and controlling glucose regulation.
- ***Metabolic Health:*** Berberine is often used to support overall metabolic function, making it a good choice if you're aiming for more efficient energy use or improved digestion.
- ***Weight Management:*** If you're trying to lose or maintain weight, berberine can support your efforts by regulating appetite and helping to balance hormones related to metabolism.
- ***Heart Health:*** Berberine may assist in reducing cholesterol levels or supporting healthy blood pressure, making it a solid choice for boosting cardiovascular wellness.
- ***Gut and Liver Health:*** Some people use berberine to promote gut health by supporting a healthy microbial balance, or to aid in liver function.

Once you identify your primary goal, write it down. Be specific and set measurable outcomes. For instance, instead of writing, "I want to lose weight," frame it as, "I aim to lose 10 pounds in three months by combining berberine with dietary changes and exercise."

2. **Understand the Importance of Writing Down Goals**

   Writing down your objectives creates a sense of commitment and reinforces your focus. It helps you turn abstract intentions into tangible targets. Consider using a notebook or a goal-setting app to record your goals and track progress over time. For example:

   - Create a checklist of your goals for better clarity.
   - Note what success looks like for you—whether it's a specific blood sugar range, a desired weight, or improved cholesterol levels.
   - Break larger goals into smaller, actionable steps. For example, if your goal is to improve metabolic health, one step might be to track your diet or incorporate 30 minutes of physical activity daily.

   Having written records makes it easier to reflect on your achievements and identify areas where you might need to make changes.

3. **Consult a Healthcare Provider**

   Talking to a doctor or healthcare professional is a vital step before starting berberine, especially if you're managing chronic health issues. A professional can help you define realistic goals and ensure berberine aligns with your needs. Here's why it's important:

- ***Personalized Advice:*** Everyone's body reacts differently, so a healthcare provider can recommend the right dosage and strategy for you.
- ***Potential Interactions:*** They can identify potential interactions with any current medications, such as blood sugar regulators, cholesterol-lowering drugs, or antibiotics.
- ***Medical Conditions:*** If you have conditions like diabetes, heart disease, or liver issues, professional guidance is essential to avoid side effects or complications.

Prepare for your consultation by making a list of your current medications, supplements, and health concerns to share with your healthcare provider.

4. Conduct Your Own Research

While professional advice is key, doing some homework on berberine's benefits and applications can empower you to make informed decisions. Consider the following steps:

- Read about how berberine works and its potential effects on conditions like insulin resistance, weight management, or cholesterol levels.

- Look into studies or articles that discuss its benefits and limitations for your specific goals.
- Choose reputable sources, such as medical websites or published studies, to ensure you're getting accurate information.

Having a well-rounded understanding will allow you to approach your berberine routine with confidence.

5. **Track Your Progress Over Time**

Once you've identified your goals and begun using berberine, tracking your progress will help you stay on track. Here's how you can do it:

- *Log Your Health Metrics:* Track key data points like blood sugar levels, weight, or blood pressure, depending on your goals. You can use health journals, apps, or spreadsheets for organization.
- *Note Changes in Symptoms:* If you're using berberine for general wellness, take note of how you feel. For instance, do you have more energy, improved digestion, or fewer sugar cravings?
- *Review Monthly or Quarterly:* Periodically assess your results. Have you made progress toward your objectives, or do you need to adjust

your approach? Use this time to fine-tune your routine or consult your doctor for advice.

Clear health goals are the foundation of a successful berberine experience. Whether you're aiming to stabilize blood sugar, lose weight, or improve heart health, knowing why you're using berberine helps you stay focused and committed. Write down your objectives, consult a trusted healthcare provider, and monitor your progress over time. By taking these steps, you'll be well on your way to reaching your health goals while using berberine.

Step 2: Start with the Right Dosage

Starting with the right dosage is essential to ensure you experience the benefits of berberine without unnecessary side effects. Berberine is a potent compound, so taking a thoughtful, gradual approach is key to maximizing its effects while allowing your body to adjust. Here's a breakdown to help you get started:

1. **Begin with a Low Dose**

    If you're new to berberine, start on the lower end of the recommended dosage range. Most experts suggest beginning at 500 mg per dose, taken two to three times a day. This typically amounts to a daily total of 1,000 to 1,500 mg. Breaking up your doses ensures your body absorbs the supplement more efficiently and helps prevent overwhelming your system.

- ***Why Start Low?*** Berberine is known for its strong effect on your digestion and metabolism. Starting with a modest dose allows your body to adapt, reducing the likelihood of side effects like stomach upset or cramping.
- ***How to Adjust Gradually?*** If you find that you tolerate the initial dose well, you can slowly increase it in small increments. For instance, after a week or two, you might raise your dosage to 750 mg per dose or three doses per day, depending on your health goals.

2. **Time Your Doses Strategically**

To get the most out of berberine, timing is everything. It works best when taken shortly before meals. Here's why:

- ***Improved Absorption:*** Taking berberine before meals enhances its bioavailability, meaning your body can absorb and use it more effectively.
- ***Blood Sugar Support:*** When taken before eating, berberine can help manage the blood sugar spikes that often happen post-meal, particularly after consuming carbohydrates.
- ***Suggested Routine:*** If you're taking berberine three times a day, aim for doses around breakfast, lunch, and dinner. Set reminders on

your phone or integrate it into your meal prep routine to make this habit consistent.

3. **Watch for Potential Side Effects**

   While berberine is generally well-tolerated, some people may experience mild side effects, particularly during the adjustment period. Here are the most common ones and how to handle them:

   - ***Digestive Discomfort:*** Symptoms such as nausea, bloating, diarrhea, or cramping can occur, especially if you start with a high dosage. To minimize this, scale back to a smaller dose, such as 250 mg per meal, and increase gradually over the weeks.
   - ***Fatigue or Mild Dizziness:*** Some people report these side effects when they first begin. If you notice them, ensure you're not skipping meals and that you're staying hydrated.
   - ***When to Seek Guidance:*** If side effects persist or worsen, it's essential to consult your healthcare provider for further advice. Severe reactions are rare but shouldn't be ignored.

4. **Check the Label and Prioritize Quality**

   With many different berberine supplements on the market, it's important to choose a high-quality product. Look for supplements that meet these standards:

- ***Third-Party Testing:*** Always select brands that have undergone independent third-party testing to ensure their products meet high standards of purity, potency, and safety. This testing provides an extra layer of assurance that you're getting exactly what the label claims.
- ***Clear Instructions:*** Look for supplements with clear, easy-to-understand dosing instructions on the label. These guidelines are typically based on expert recommendations and should be followed carefully unless a healthcare professional advises otherwise. Proper dosing helps you achieve the desired benefits while minimizing risks.
- ***No Unnecessary Additives:*** Opt for products free from fillers, artificial colors, flavors, or preservatives that may reduce the supplement's quality or cause unwanted side effects. High-quality supplements focus on delivering active ingredients without unnecessary additives that don't support your health goals.

5. Consult a Healthcare Professional

Although berberine is a natural supplement, it's always wise to talk to your healthcare provider before starting, especially if you:

- Have existing health conditions like diabetes, heart disease, or liver issues.
- Are pregnant, nursing, or planning to conceive.
- Take medications such as blood sugar regulators, blood pressure meds, or antibiotics, as berberine can interact with some drugs.

Your healthcare provider can help tailor the dosage to your specific needs, ensuring safe and effective use of berberine.

6. Monitor Your Body's Response

Pay attention to how your body reacts to berberine in the first few weeks. Keeping a log of any side effects, changes in energy levels, or progress in your health objectives can help you understand how the supplement is working for you. For instance:

- If You're Managing Blood Sugar: Check your blood sugar levels before and after meals (if you have a testing device) to see how berberine is affecting them.
- If Your Primary Goal is Weight Loss or Metabolism Support: Track your weight and note how your appetite or energy levels shift over time.

This insight will help you and your healthcare provider adjust your routine for long-term success.

Starting with the right dosage of berberine is about being smart and patient. Ease into it with lower doses, take it consistently with meals for better absorption, and pay close attention to what your body tells you. By keeping these steps in mind, you'll set yourself up for success as you explore the potential benefits of berberine in your health routine.

Step 3: Pair Berberine with Diet and Lifestyle Changes

To maximize the potential of berberine, it's essential to pair it with meaningful diet and lifestyle changes. Think of berberine as a key player in your health routine, but not the sole solution—it works best when partnered with consistent, healthy habits. Here's how you can make those changes:

1. **Optimize Your Diet**

    A well-balanced, nutrient-rich diet is one of the most important factors in achieving your health goals. Here's how to adjust your food choices for maximum results with berberine:

    - ***Focus on Whole Foods:*** Incorporate fresh, whole foods into your meals. Aim for vegetables like leafy greens, broccoli, cauliflower, and peppers, which are rich in vitamins and minerals and low in calories.

- ***Prioritize Fiber:*** Foods high in fiber, such as oats, lentils, chia seeds, flaxseeds, and berries, can further help regulate blood sugar while promoting healthy digestion.
- ***Choose Lean Proteins:*** Include options like chicken, turkey, tofu, eggs, or fish (especially fatty fish like salmon and mackerel, which are rich in omega-3s). Proteins help stabilize blood sugar and keep you feeling full for longer.
- ***Add Healthy Fats:*** Healthy fats, such as avocados, nuts, seeds, and olive oil, play a vital role in supporting your metabolic health.
- ***Reduce Sugary and Processed Foods:*** Minimize refined sugars, sugary drinks like soda, and pastries, and processed snacks such as chips and packaged baked goods. These can spike blood sugar levels and reduce the positive effects of berberine.

To make these habits sustainable, try meal prepping on weekends, creating balanced plates with protein, fiber, and fats for every meal, or swapping sugary desserts for natural sweets like fruit.

2. **Step Up Your Physical Activity**

   While berberine is known for its ability to support metabolic health, pairing it with exercise can supercharge its effects. Regular movement helps improve insulin sensitivity, manage weight, and keep your heart healthy. Here's how you can start or enhance your activity level:

- ***Start Simple:*** If you're new to exercise, begin with daily walks. Aim for 30 minutes each day, which could be broken into smaller chunks if needed. Walking after meals is especially effective for stabilizing blood sugar levels.
- ***Explore Strength Training:*** Building muscle through activities like weightlifting, bodyweight exercises, or resistance bands can improve your metabolism and support long-term health. You don't need a gym—bodyweight squats, push-ups, and resistance band exercises work wonders at home.
- ***Find What You Love:*** Whether it's yoga, cycling, or a group dance class, pick an activity that excites you. When exercise feels like fun, consistency becomes natural.
- ***Look for Everyday Opportunities:*** Don't underestimate small changes like taking the stairs, parking farther from your destination, or doing quick stretches while watching TV. These seemingly minor adjustments add up over time.

3. **Build Healthy Habits into Your Routine**

Making sustainable changes is all about consistency and finding ways to fit better choices into your everyday life. A few practical tips include:

- ***Schedule Your Meals and Activity:*** Eating at regular times and scheduling exercise into your day helps you stay consistent.
- ***Track Your Choices:*** Use a food journal or an app to monitor what you're eating and how often you're moving. Awareness can motivate smarter decisions.
- ***Plan for Success:*** When you know you have a busy day ahead, pack healthy snacks like nuts or fresh veggies to avoid resorting to fast food or vending machines. Similarly, set out walking shoes or workout clothes as a visual cue to stay active.
- ***Stay Hydrated:*** Drinking plenty of water is essential for overall health and metabolism. Aim for 8-10 glasses per day, and substitute sugary drinks with options like herbal tea or sparkling water with a squeeze of lemon.

4. **Commitment to Consistency**

The key to unlocking berberine's true potential lies in your ability to stick with these habits over time. These adjustments may feel challenging at first, but small, steady improvements count far more than radical changes you can't sustain. Focus on setting long-term goals and celebrating milestones—every bit of progress matters, no matter how small.

By pairing berberine with a thoughtful approach to diet and lifestyle, you're not only enhancing its benefits but also building a foundation for lasting health.

Step 4: Monitor Your Progress

Monitoring your progress is a crucial step to understanding whether berberine is working for you and helping you achieve your health goals. By paying attention to measurable changes in your body and keeping track of how you feel, you can fine-tune your routine for maximum benefits. Here's how to stay on top of your progress:

1. **Track Key Health Metrics**

   Depending on your goals, there are specific health indicators you'll want to monitor to gauge berberine's effectiveness. Here are some examples:

   - *Blood Sugar Levels:* If managing blood sugar is your goal, use a glucose monitoring device to check your levels before and after meals. Keep an eye on patterns, such as whether your fasting blood sugar reduces over time.

- *Weight Management:* For those focusing on weight loss or maintenance, weigh yourself weekly and measure your waistline or body fat percentage for a more complete picture.
- *Cholesterol and Heart Health:* If your focus is on improving cholesterol or triglyceride levels, periodic blood tests can show how berberine is affecting your lipid profile.
- *Energy and Digestive Health:* Take note of how your energy levels fluctuate or whether digestion feels smoother, especially if berberine is part of a gut health plan.

Tracking these data points consistently will help you understand trends and measure tangible results.

2. Keep a Health Journal

A health journal can be a simple yet powerful tool for documenting your berberine experience. Here's what you can include and how it can help:

- *Daily Log:* Record the dosage and times you take berberine, along with notes on meals or snacks. For example, track whether you took it before meals and list basic details about your food choices.
- *Physical Changes:* Note any changes in your weight, digestion, energy levels, or physical

symptoms like bloating or fatigue. Be specific—details like "more energy after meals" or "reduced sugar cravings" can highlight progress.

- ***Mood and Mental Health:*** Since metabolic health can influence your mood, jot down how you're feeling emotionally and mentally. Are you more focused or less irritable? Recording this information can help detect subtle but meaningful improvements.

Journaling not only helps you stay accountable but also gives you a comprehensive view of how your body reacts to berberine over time. Consider using a physical notebook or a digital app to keep everything organized.

3. Use Monitoring Tools and Tests

For more precise tracking, leverage tools like blood tests or home monitoring devices. These can provide valuable data points beyond how you're feeling.

- ***Blood Sugar Monitoring Tools:*** Portable glucometers allow you to easily check your blood sugar levels from the comfort of home. Make it a habit to test at consistent times, such as before breakfast (fasting) or two hours after meals.

- *Cholesterol Tests:* If heart health is a priority, regular blood work performed by your doctor can track markers like HDL ("good" cholesterol), LDL ("bad" cholesterol), and triglycerides.
- *Body Composition Scales:* Advanced scales that measure metrics like fat percentage and muscle mass can be helpful if you're monitoring weight loss or metabolic changes.

Be sure to routinely compare your results against your original goals. For instance, if your fasting blood sugar initially measured 120 mg/dL and drops to below 100 mg/dL, it's a clear indicator that berberine may be making a positive impact.

4. **Adjust Based on Results**

Your progress data isn't just for motivation—it's also essential for refining your routine. Regular evaluations will help you determine whether adjustments to dosage, diet, or lifestyle are needed:

- *If Progress Is Slow:* Consider checking in with your healthcare provider to revisit your dosage. It may be that you need to optimize when or how much berberine you take.
- *If You Encounter Side Effects:* Use your journal to note when side effects occur. For

instance, if stomach upset happens after higher doses, adjusting to smaller doses may help.
- ***Plateaus in Results:*** If weight loss or improvements in blood sugar plateau, evaluate other habits that could be holding you back, such as inconsistent exercise or unbalanced meals.

Flexibility is key to finding the routine that works best for you.

5. **Stay Motivated with Progress Tracking**

Celebrating small victories along the way can keep you motivated and focused. Here are ways to stay inspired:

- ***Visualize Progress:*** Use graphs, charts, or tracking apps to monitor your journey and observe trends over time, such as improvements in fasting blood sugar levels, steady weight loss, or reduced cholesterol. Seeing these patterns can help you understand how far you've come and make abstract numbers feel more meaningful and rewarding. Visualizing progress can also motivate you to stay consistent with your routine.
- ***Celebrate Milestones:*** Break your larger goals into smaller, achievable mini-goals and celebrate when you reach them. For example,

reward yourself with a new workout outfit, a relaxing massage, or a night out with friends after hitting your weight target or improving your lab results. Acknowledging these achievements reinforces positive habits and gives you something to look forward to during your journey.

- ***Reflect on Changes:*** Take time to compare how you felt before starting Berberine to how you feel now. Maybe your energy is more sustained throughout the day, you're sleeping better at night, or your cravings for unhealthy snacks have decreased. These subtle improvements might be easy to overlook without reflection, so consider journaling your thoughts or sharing your wins with a friend to fully appreciate the progress you've made.

Monitoring your progress ensures you're on the right track and getting the most from berberine. It also helps you make data-driven decisions about your health. Whether you're recording your daily doses, noting subtle improvements in energy, or tracking larger health metrics like blood sugar or cholesterol levels, this habit will bring clarity and direction to your health journey.

Progress tracking not only lets you see how far you've come but also empowers you to make adjustments that unlock the full potential of your efforts alongside berberine.

Step 5: Adjust Your Routine for Long-Term Benefits

After taking berberine for a few weeks or months, you'll have a better sense of how it fits into your lifestyle and supports your health goals. Long-term success with berberine isn't just about starting strong—it's about staying consistent and adaptable. Here's how to adjust your routine for sustainable results:

1. **Fine-Tune Your Dosage**

    Once your body has adjusted to berberine, you may find it beneficial to make small tweaks to your dosage based on your health needs and goals.

    Increasing Gradually:

    If you tolerate your current dose well and haven't reached the desired results, consider increasing your dosage slightly while staying within the recommended limits (e.g., 500 mg two to three times daily).

    Gradual increases not only help you find the right balance but also minimize the risk of unwanted side effects like digestive discomfort. It's important to monitor how your body responds to any changes and consult with a healthcare professional if you're unsure about the appropriate dosage for your needs. Patience and caution are key when adjusting your intake.

Splitting Doses:

If you're experiencing inconsistent results or side effects from your current dosing schedule, consider adjusting the timing or distribution of doses. For example, instead of taking two larger doses in the morning and evening, you might try splitting them into three smaller doses spread throughout the day before meals.

This can help improve absorption and maintain more consistent levels in your system, potentially enhancing the medication's effectiveness and reducing unwanted side effects.

Consult Your Healthcare Provider:

Before making any significant changes to your dosing schedule, it's crucial to consult your healthcare provider. They can help you determine the best approach based on your unique health needs, current medications, and overall treatment plan.

Your doctor's guidance ensures any adjustments are safe and won't interfere with other medications or conditions you may have. Taking this step can help you stay on track toward achieving your health goals.

Fine-tuning means personalizing the routine to meet your unique needs while ensuring safety and effectiveness.

2. **Adapt to Evolving Health Goals**

   Health is not a static process. Over time, your objectives may change, requiring you to adjust your approach to taking berberine.

   Reassess Initial Goals:

   If you initially started taking berberine with a goal like weight loss and have successfully achieved it, it's time to pivot and focus on maintaining those results. This could mean pairing berberine with ongoing lifestyle habits, such as a balanced diet, regular exercise, and stress management, to keep your metabolism running efficiently. Reflect on what has worked so far and build a plan to sustain your progress over the long term.

   Shifting Priorities:

   As your health journey evolves, you might find new goals taking precedence. For example, you may want to focus on managing your blood sugar levels, improving cholesterol, or supporting gut health.

To make the most of berberine, track metrics related to these new objectives, such as blood tests, energy levels, or digestion. Use this information to tailor your routine by incorporating other supportive habits or adjustments to your diet and supplement schedule.

Think Long Term:

Health is about the big picture, and berberine can play a key role in your broader wellness strategy. Think about how it fits alongside other tools for maintaining health, such as additional supplements, medications, or preventive care like regular check-ups and screenings.

As your needs shift with age or lifestyle changes, remain open to evolving your approach. Consider consulting with a healthcare provider to ensure berberine continues to align with your long-term wellness goals.

Revisiting your goals keeps your berberine routine purposeful and aligned with your changing needs.

3. **Maintain Consistency**

The key to harnessing berberine's long-term benefits is consistency. Regular use ensures your body continues to adapt and respond to the supplement. Create habits that make taking berberine as routine as brushing your teeth or drinking your morning coffee.

- **Set Reminders:** Use alarms, sticky notes, or smartphone notifications to remind you to take berberine at consistent times each day, ideally before meals for optimal absorption.
- **Combine with Existing Habits:** Pair berberine with something you already do daily. For example, take your dose right after brewing your morning coffee or just before sitting down to lunch.
- **Prepare Ahead:** If you're often on the go, portion out doses in travel-friendly containers so you never have to skip a dose. This is especially helpful for those with busy lifestyles or frequent travel.

By weaving berberine into your daily routine, it becomes less of a task and more of a seamless habit.

4. **Revisit Your Progress Regularly**

Periodic check-ins help you evaluate whether your current approach is working and whether it's time to pivot. Aim to reassess your progress every three to six months.

- **Review Key Metrics:** Whether it's blood sugar, cholesterol levels, or weight, compare your current numbers to your starting point. Look for

trends to assess progress, plateaus, or areas of concern.
- ***Feedback from Journals:*** If you've been keeping a health journal, review past entries to spot patterns. For example, you might notice that increasing your dose coincided with improved energy levels.
- ***Seek Professional Input:*** Schedule a follow-up visit with your healthcare provider to review your numbers and discuss whether adjustments are needed to your dosage, routine, or health goals.

Frequent reassessments ensure you stay on track and make smarter, more informed decisions.

5. Ensure Continued Effectiveness

Berberine can remain a valuable part of your wellness strategy for the long term when paired with healthy habits. Over time, you may need to adjust not just your dosage but also other aspects of your lifestyle for sustained results.

- ***Pair with Balanced Nutrition:*** A nutrient-rich diet continues to amplify berberine's benefits. Focus on whole foods, lean proteins, and healthy fats while limiting highly processed items.

- *Stay Physically Active:* Berberine's metabolic support works best with regular exercise. Whether it's walking after meals, strength training, or yoga, find movement you enjoy to maintain a sustainable fitness habit.
- *Monitor for Changes:* Bodies and lifestyles change over time. Pay attention to how you feel and periodically evaluate whether your current routine is still effective based on your needs.

With consistent effort and periodic adaptations, you can integrate berberine into a holistic approach to health.

Adjusting your berberine routine as needed allows you to stay aligned with your goals while adapting to your body's changing needs. Start with small, intentional changes—whether it's tweaking your dosage, adjusting your habits, or shifting your focus—and always keep consistency at the heart of your approach. By taking the time to periodically reassess and fine-tune, you'll ensure that berberine continues to support your health for the long haul.

Enhancing Results with Lifestyle Changes

Berberine can be an effective tool in supporting blood sugar regulation, weight management, and overall health, but its benefits are magnified when combined with thoughtful lifestyle adjustments. This chapter explores how dietary choices, exercise habits, stress management, and sleep play vital roles in enhancing the effects of Berberine. By taking a holistic approach to your well-being, you can optimize your results and create sustainable changes for long-term health.

Dietary Tips for Blood Sugar and Weight Management

Your diet is one of the most influential factors in managing blood sugar levels and achieving weight loss goals. Adding Berberine to a nutrient-rich, balanced diet can amplify its effects.

1. **Build a Balanced Plate**

    Focus on meals that include fiber, lean protein, and healthy fats. These three components stabilize blood sugar levels by slowing glucose absorption and keeping you full longer. Here's how to structure your meals:

- ***Fiber-Rich Foods:*** Incorporate vegetables like leafy greens, broccoli, and zucchini, as well as whole grains such as quinoa or oats. Fiber helps slow digestion and prevents rapid blood sugar spikes.
- ***Lean Proteins:*** Add grilled chicken, fish, turkey, tofu, or legumes to your meals to promote satiety and muscle health.
- ***Healthy Fats:*** Include avocado, nuts, seeds, and olive oil, which support hormone production and reduce inflammation.

For example, a balanced lunch might include baked salmon, roasted asparagus, and a side of quinoa topped with avocado slices.

2. Avoid Problematic Foods

Certain foods can undermine both your health goals and the effects of Berberine by causing blood sugar spikes or contributing to weight gain:

- ***Sugary Drinks and Desserts:*** Minimize intake of soda, candy, pastries, and other high-sugar items that provide empty calories.

- ***Refined Carbs:*** White bread, pastas, and processed snacks are quickly broken down into glucose, leading to sharp blood sugar fluctuations.
- ***Highly Processed Foods:*** Packaged meals or snacks often contain trans fats, high sodium, and added sugars, hindering metabolic health.

Replace these items with nutrient-dense alternatives. For instance, swap soda for sparkling water with lemon or chips for roasted chickpeas.

3. Practice Portion Control

Controlling portion sizes is key for regulating calorie intake. Use smaller plates, measure servings, and eat mindfully to prevent overeating. For example, stop eating when you feel 80% full, allowing your body time to signal fullness.

4. Time Your Meals

If your goal is to stabilize blood sugar, eating smaller, frequent meals throughout the day can be beneficial. Try not to skip meals, as this can result in cravings and unstable glucose levels, leading to energy crashes. Pairing meals with your Berberine doses (e.g., before meals) can further enhance its effects.

By making deliberate dietary choices, you can support your body's natural ability to balance blood sugar and achieve your goals.

Exercise Recommendations to Boost Metabolism

Physical activity works synergistically with Berberine to improve metabolic health, manage weight, and regulate blood sugar. Integrating exercise into your routine doesn't have to mean spending hours at the gym—it's about finding what suits your lifestyle and sticking to it.

1. **Strength Training for Muscle Growth**

   Strength training builds lean muscle mass, which increases your resting metabolic rate and improves insulin sensitivity. Aim for resistance training exercises like:

   - Bodyweight exercises (push-ups, squats, lunges)
   - Weightlifting (using free weights or machines)
   - Resistance bands for a low-impact option

   Begin with two to three strength-training sessions per week, gradually building intensity. For example, a beginner might start with 15-minute sessions of bodyweight exercises, increasing duration over time.

2. Cardiovascular Exercise for Fat Burning

Cardio exercises are essential for burning calories and improving heart health. Options range from low-intensity activities like walking to higher-intensity workouts like running or cycling.

- *High-Intensity Interval Training (HIIT):* If you're short on time, try HIIT. These workouts involve alternating between short bursts of all-out effort and slower recovery periods. For instance, sprint for 30 seconds, walk for 1 minute, and repeat this cycle for 15-20 minutes.
- *Daily Movement:* Make small changes, such as taking the stairs instead of the elevator or walking during phone calls, to integrate movement into your day-to-day routine.

3. Post-Meal Walks

Walking for just 10-15 minutes after meals can significantly enhance glucose metabolism. This activity prompts your muscles to use glucose for energy, decreasing blood sugar spikes.

4. Stay Consistent

The best exercise plan is one you enjoy and can stick to. Try different activities to find what motivates you—dance classes, yoga, swimming, or even gardening can double as exercise. Aim for at least 150 minutes of moderate activity per week alongside two strength sessions.

By coupling regular physical activity with Berberine, you'll boost your metabolism, improve your body's response to insulin, and feel more energetic.

Stress Management and Sleep Optimization

Reducing stress and improving sleep quality are often overlooked but essential aspects of metabolic health. Chronic stress and poor sleep can undermine the positive effects of Berberine by elevating cortisol levels, impairing insulin sensitivity, and disrupting appetite regulation.

1. **Manage Stress Effectively**

   Stress can lead to emotional eating, weight gain, and unstable blood sugar levels. Incorporate daily habits to reduce stress and promote relaxation:

   - *Mindfulness Practices:* Try meditation or deep-breathing exercises for a few minutes each day to calm the mind and lower cortisol levels. Apps like Headspace or Calm can help guide beginners.
   - *Exercise:* Stress-reducing activities like yoga, tai chi, or even gentle stretching can have calming effects.

- ***Engage in Hobbies:*** Dedicate time to activities you love, be it painting, gardening, reading, or playing an instrument.

Learning to manage stress gives your body the best chance to function optimally.

2. **Prioritize High-Quality Sleep**

Sleep is when your body repairs and regulates hormones that control appetite and metabolism. Aim for 7-9 hours of restful sleep per night by following these tips:

- ***Maintain a Sleep Schedule:*** Go to bed and wake up at the same time daily, even on weekends. This regulates your body's internal clock.
- ***Create a Sleep-Friendly Environment:*** Keep your bedroom cool, dark, and quiet. Remove distractions like electronics, and consider blackout curtains or white noise machines.
- ***Wind Down Before Bed:*** Avoid screens and intense mental activities an hour before sleeping. Opt for relaxing activities like reading or taking a warm bath.
- ***Monitor Caffeine Consumption:*** Limit caffeine intake in the afternoon and evening, as it can disrupt sleep cycles.

By improving sleep quality, your body will be better equipped to maintain healthy blood sugar levels, metabolize food efficiently, and manage weight.

3. **Check in Regularly**

    Make stress management and sleep tracking part of your overall health routine. Use a journal or app to note stress triggers or monitor the quality of your sleep over time. Small habits, like recognizing stress or adjusting your bedtime routine, can have a big impact.

    Enhancing your results with lifestyle changes means creating a strong foundation that amplifies the benefits of Berberine. A balanced diet, regular exercise, stress management, and good sleep hygiene all work together to support overall well-being.

Remember, progress builds over time, so stay consistent and adaptable as you work towards a healthier, more energized you. By adopting a holistic approach, you're not only maximizing Berberine's effects—you're creating habits for lifelong health.

Potential Side Effects and How to Handle Them

While berberine is widely recognized for its health benefits, some individuals may experience mild side effects when starting supplementation. Knowing what to expect, how to manage side effects, and when to consult a healthcare provider will ensure a safe and positive experience with berberine.

Digestive Upset

One of the most frequently reported side effects of berberine is mild digestive discomfort, especially in the initial stages of supplementation.

Symptoms May Include:

- Bloating
- Gas
- Stomach cramps
- Diarrhea or loose stools

Why It Happens:

Berberine has antimicrobial properties that may alter gut bacteria, leading to temporary changes as your body adjusts. Higher doses can also overwhelm the digestive system early on.

What to Do:

- Start with a low dose, such as 500 mg once a day, to allow your body to adapt gradually.
- Take berberine with meals. This can help mitigate stomach irritation by slowing absorption.
- Stay hydrated to replenish fluids in case of diarrhea.

When to Expect Relief:

These symptoms typically subside within a week or two as your body adjusts. However, if digestive discomfort persists, consider a smaller dose or speak with your healthcare provider.

Lowered Blood Sugar

Because berberine can effectively reduce blood sugar levels, some individuals (especially those taking diabetes medications) may experience blood sugar dropping too low, a condition known as hypoglycemia.

Symptoms May Include:

- Dizziness
- Shakiness
- Weakness or fatigue
- Sweating

What to Do:

- Monitor your blood sugar levels regularly if you have a history of diabetes or low blood sugar.
- Ensure you're eating balanced meals to maintain stable glucose levels.
- If you notice symptoms of hypoglycemia, consume a quick source of sugar, such as fruit juice or a small portion of candy.

When to Seek Help:

If low blood sugar episodes occur frequently, consult your healthcare provider. They may recommend adjusting the dosage or monitoring your medications more closely.

Allergic Reactions

Though rare, some individuals may experience an allergic reaction to berberine or its components.

Symptoms May Include:

- An itchy rash or hives
- Swelling (especially of the face or throat)
- Difficulty breathing

What to Do:

- Stop taking berberine immediately if you suspect an allergic reaction.
- Use over-the-counter antihistamines for mild reactions, but call your doctor if symptoms persist.
- Seek emergency medical care if you experience severe swelling or difficulty breathing.

Practical Tips for Managing Mild Side Effects

To minimize the risk of side effects, consider these tips when taking berberine:

- *Stay Consistent:* Side effects are often temporary and may resolve as your body adapts. Stick with a consistent routine for a week or two before making changes.
- *Adjust the Dose Gradually:* If transitioning to a higher dosage, do so in small increments over time to minimize any shock to your system.
- *Choose High-Quality Formulations:* Select supplements from trusted brands to avoid additives, fillers, or impurities that could exacerbate side effects.
- *Pair with Food:* Taking berberine alongside meals not only aids in digestion but also reduces the chance of nausea or irritation.

Overall, berberine is considered safe for most individuals. However, as with any supplement or medication, it's important to be aware of potential side effects and seek help if necessary. By following these practical tips and monitoring your body's response, you can safely incorporate berberine into your healthcare routine. Remember to always consult with a healthcare professional before starting any new supplement or making changes to your current regimen.

When to Consult a Doctor

Knowing when to consult a healthcare provider is essential to ensure your safety while supplementing with berberine.

1. **Persistent or Severe Digestive Issues**

    If symptoms like diarrhea, cramping, or bloating last longer than two weeks or are severe enough to disrupt your daily life, it's time to seek professional advice.

2. **Low Blood Sugar Episodes**

    Frequent hypoglycemia, dizziness, or shakiness that doesn't improve with dietary adjustments warrants medical attention. These symptoms could indicate that berberine is interacting with medications or that dosage adjustments are necessary.

3. **Existing Health Conditions**

   If you have liver disease, kidney problems, or are pregnant, it's important to consult a healthcare provider before starting berberine. Certain medical conditions may require more careful management or could make berberine unsuitable for your health.

4. **Medication Interactions**

   Berberine can interact with certain medications, such as blood thinners, blood pressure medications, and antibiotics. Consult a healthcare provider if you're on prescribed medications to avoid potential complications.

5. **Symptoms of Allergy or Severe Reaction**

   For any signs of an allergic reaction (rash, severe swelling, or breathing difficulty), stop taking berberine immediately and seek medical care.

Monitoring Your Health

Being proactive and mindful while taking berberine is key to minimizing side effects.

- Keep a health journal to track how your body responds, including any symptoms or improvements.

- Regular blood work (e.g., blood sugar, and liver function tests) can help you and your healthcare provider monitor progress and ensure long-term safety.
- Address any concerns promptly rather than waiting for minor issues to escalate.

Berberine is generally safe and effective, but as with any supplement, side effects can occur. By starting with small doses, monitoring your body's response, and consulting your doctor when necessary, you can use berberine confidently while maximizing its health benefits. Listen to your body, adjust as needed, and always prioritize your overall well-being.

Avoiding Pitfalls and Maximizing Benefits

To get the most out of berberine supplementation and ensure its safe use, it's crucial to focus on proper timing, frequency of doses, and understanding possible interactions with medications. With a thoughtful approach, you can sidestep common mistakes and fully reap the health benefits berberine has to offer.

Timing and Frequency of Doses

When and how often you take berberine can significantly impact its effectiveness and minimize the risk of side effects.

1. **Divide Your Doses Throughout the Day**

    Berberine has a relatively short half-life, meaning it doesn't stay in your system for very long. To maintain steady levels in your body, divide your daily dose into two or three smaller doses.

- *Example:* If your total daily dose is 1,500 mg, you could take 500 mg with breakfast, lunch, and dinner.
- *Why It's Important:* Dividing doses ensures consistent absorption and helps prevent digestive discomfort caused by taking too much at once.

2. **Take Berberine With Meals**

Berberine is best absorbed with food, and taking it with meals can also reduce the risk of digestive upset.

- *Meals to Prioritize:* Taking berberine alongside your largest or most carbohydrate-heavy meals may help stabilize post-meal glucose levels.
- *Why It Works:* When you eat, your blood sugar naturally rises, and berberine helps regulate how your body processes and stores that glucose.

Tip: Pair berberine doses with your regular meal times to make it easier to remember and establish a consistent habit.

3. **Avoid Taking It Too Close to Bedtime**

For some individuals, berberine may slightly boost energy levels or make digestion more active. To prevent potential sleep disruptions, schedule your last dose at least two to three hours before going to bed.

Tip: Observe your body's response and adjust timing if needed to promote the best balance between energy and rest.

Interactions with Medications

Berberine is a potent supplement that can interact with various medications. Understanding these interactions is vital for avoiding adverse effects and ensuring your health is protected.

1. **Blood Sugar Medications**

    Berberine lowers blood sugar, which can compound the effects of medications such as insulin or oral hypoglycemics (e.g., metformin). This may lead to episodes of low blood sugar (hypoglycemia).

    - *Risk:* Symptoms of hypoglycemia include dizziness, sweating, and shakiness.
    - *Solution:* If you're taking diabetes medications, check blood sugar levels regularly and discuss dosage adjustments with your healthcare provider. You may need to modify either your medication or berberine dose for safe and effective use.

2. **Blood Thinners**

   Berberine may have a mild blood-thinning effect, leading to potential interactions with anticoagulants such as warfarin or aspirin.

   - *Risk:* It could increase the risk of bleeding or bruising.
   - *Solution:* Inform your doctor if you're taking anticoagulants and want to start berberine. They can monitor your blood and adjust medication as needed.

3. **Blood Pressure Medications**

   Berberine has been shown to lower blood pressure, which could amplify the effects of antihypertensive drugs like beta-blockers or ACE inhibitors.

   - *Risk:* This combination might cause dizziness or lightheadedness due to blood pressure dropping too low.
   - *Solution:* Work with your healthcare provider to monitor blood pressure closely when adding berberine to your routine.

4. **Antibiotics**

   Berberine has natural antimicrobial properties, which may interfere with certain antibiotics by altering gut flora.

- **Risk:** This could reduce the effectiveness of antibiotics or disrupt gut health.
- **Solution:** If you're prescribed antibiotics, ask your doctor whether it's safe to temporarily pause berberine supplementation.

5. **Liver-Enzyme Interactions**

Berberine is metabolized by enzymes in the liver (like CYP3A4), which are also responsible for processing many medications, such as statins and antidepressants.

- **Risk:** Taking berberine alongside these drugs might either reduce their effectiveness or amplify their concentration in your system, increasing the risk of side effects.
- **Solution:** Your healthcare provider can help assess whether berberine is compatible with your medications.

Key Tip: Always provide your doctor with a complete list of medications and supplements you're taking before starting berberine. This will help them identify any potential risks early on.

Practical Advice for Avoiding Pitfalls

1. **Communicate With Your Healthcare Provider**

Before starting berberine, schedule a consultation with your doctor, especially if you're already taking medications or have ongoing health conditions such as diabetes or heart disease.

Why It Matters:

- They can recommend the safest dosage and schedule based on your unique health profile.
- Laboratory tests can establish baseline health markers (e.g., blood sugar, cholesterol) to monitor progress and avoid complications.

2. Monitor Your Body's Response

Keep a journal to track any changes in how you feel, including improvements or side effects like digestive upset or fatigue. This will help you identify issues early and recognize positive trends.

Tip: Log information like the timing of doses, meals, exercise, and any noticeable changes in energy levels or well-being. Sharing this with your doctor during check-ins can provide helpful insights.

3. Follow Recommended Dosages

Avoid taking more berberine than recommended, as higher doses do not necessarily lead to faster results and may increase the chance of side effects.

Tip: If you're unsure about the right dose, start low, monitor your response, and adjust gradually with professional guidance.

4. **Choose High-Quality Supplements**

   Select berberine supplements from reputable brands that prioritize purity and third-party testing. Poorly manufactured supplements may contain contaminants that could lead to unnecessary side effects or reduce effectiveness.

   Tip: Look for certifications like "USP Verified" or testing by independent labs on product labels or brand websites.

5. **Stay Patient**

   Berberine is not a quick fix. Lasting health improvements, such as stabilized blood sugar or healthy weight loss, are achieved over time through consistent supplementation and lifestyle adjustments.

   Tip: Stay focused on long-term outcomes rather than expecting immediate results.

Avoiding pitfalls with berberine supplementation is all about being informed and proactive. By timing your doses effectively, monitoring for medication interactions, and consulting with your healthcare provider, you can safely maximize the benefits of berberine. Take a steady approach, listen to your body, and incorporate healthy habits, and you'll be well on your way to achieving your health goals.

Conclusion

Congratulations on reaching the end of this comprehensive guide on Berberine! By taking the time to explore this natural compound, you've already made a significant step toward understanding how it can play a role in your well-being. Whether you're looking to regulate blood sugar, support weight management, improve heart health, or enhance your overall metabolic function, you now have the knowledge to make informed decisions.

Berberine is more than just a supplement; it's a tool that, when used wisely, can unlock impressive health benefits. From its ability to activate AMPK—the "metabolic master switch"—to its positive impact on blood sugar, heart health, and even hormonal balance, this powerful compound offers a natural solution to some of the most common and complex health challenges.

But here's the key takeaway to remember: Berberine isn't a magic fix. It works best when paired with consistent, positive lifestyle choices. Think of it as a support beam for your health—it holds up your efforts but cannot replace the foundation of balanced eating, regular physical activity, stress management, and quality sleep. When you combine Berberine with these habits, you're creating a solid road map to long-term wellness.

Throughout this guide, we've emphasized the importance of personalizing your approach. After all, no two wellness journeys are exactly alike. By setting clear health goals, starting with the right doses, and tracking your progress, you can ensure that Berberine fits seamlessly into your routine. This is a moment to take ownership of your health. Whether you're striving for more stable energy levels, improved labs, or even the peace of mind that comes from knowing your body is functioning more efficiently, Berberine has the potential to help along the way.

However, as with any health decision, it's vital to approach supplementation thoughtfully. Always consult with your healthcare provider before adding Berberine to your routine, especially if you're managing existing conditions or taking medications. Your doctor's input can ensure that this natural remedy aligns safely with your health profile, helping you avoid potential pitfalls and achieve optimal results.

Most importantly, be patient. True, meaningful health transformations are built over time through consistent effort. Celebrate every small step forward, whether it's a lower fasting blood sugar level, improved digestion, or simply feeling more energized throughout the day. Your progress might not always feel fast, but it will be steady—and that's what matters most.

Thank you for investing in your health by reading this guide. Your willingness to learn, adapt, and take action shows that you're serious about creating a better version of yourself. Berberine is just one piece of the wellness puzzle, but with the insights and strategies outlined here, you're equipped to fit that piece into your unique story.

Now, it's time to put what you've learned into practice. Reflect on your goals, build healthier routines, and consult the right professionals for guidance. You're capable of making incredible changes to your health—one informed choice at a time.

FAQs

Can I take Berberine long-term?

Berberine is generally considered safe for long-term use, but it's essential to take breaks periodically (e.g., after a few months of consistent use) to allow your body to reset. Long-term use should always be monitored by a healthcare professional to avoid potential interactions, side effects, or overuse.

What are the signs it's working?

If Berberine is working for you, you may notice improvements in specific health markers like better blood sugar control, reduced cholesterol levels, or improved digestion. These changes are usually confirmed through regular blood tests or noticeable physical improvements, such as steady energy levels or healthier weight management.

Who should avoid Berberine?

Berberine should be avoided by pregnant and breastfeeding women, as it may pose risks to the baby. Additionally, individuals with low blood sugar, certain liver conditions, or those taking multiple medications that interact with Berberine should consult a doctor before use.

What is Berberine and where does it come from?

Berberine is a natural alkaloid found in plants like barberry, goldenseal, and Oregon grape. Extracted from the roots, stems, and bark of these plants, it has been used for centuries in traditional medicine for its antimicrobial, anti-inflammatory, and metabolic benefits.

How does Berberine work in the body?

Berberine activates AMPK, the "metabolic master switch," which helps regulate energy balance, metabolism, and fat storage. It also improves insulin sensitivity, influences gut health, and supports blood sugar and cholesterol management, making it a versatile natural remedy.

What are the potential health benefits of Berberine?

Berberine offers several potential benefits, including better blood sugar control, lower cholesterol levels, improved digestion, balanced gut bacteria, and support for heart health. It's also being studied for its possible effects on weight management and hormonal conditions like PCOS.

Are there any side effects associated with Berberine?

Some people may experience mild side effects, such as stomach upset, diarrhea, or cramps, especially at higher doses. These effects can often be minimized by starting with smaller doses and taking Berberine with meals. Always consult a healthcare provider if side effects persist.

References and Helpful Links

BERBERINE: Overview, uses, side effects, precautions, interactions, dosing and reviews. (n.d.).
https://www.webmd.com/vitamins/ai/ingredientmono-1126/berberine

Berberine and weight loss: what you need to know. (n.d.). NCCIH.
https://www.nccih.nih.gov/health/berberine-and-weight-loss-what-you-need-to-know

BSc, K. G. (2023, June 13). Berberine – a powerful supplement with many benefits. Healthline.
https://www.healthline.com/nutrition/berberine-powerful-supplement

Berberine benefits for women – PCOS, perimenopause, and more. (n.d.). Gynecology, Integrative Medicine & Functional Medicine Located in Upper East Side, New York, NY | TāràMD.
https://www.taramd.com/post/berberine-benefits-for-women-pcos-perimenopause-and-more

Och, A., Och, M., Nowak, R., Podgórska, D., & Podgórski, R. (2022). Berberine, a herbal metabolite in the metabolic syndrome: the risk factors, course, and consequences of the disease. Molecules, 27(4), 1351. https://doi.org/10.3390/molecules27041351

Lee, Y. S., Kim, W. S., Kim, K. H., Yoon, M. J., Cho, H. J., Shen, Y., Ye, J., Lee, C. H., Oh, W. K., Kim, C. T., Hohnen-Behrens, C., Gosby, A., Kraegen, E. W., James, D. E., & Kim, J. B. (2006). Berberine, a natural plant product, activates AMP-Activated protein kinase with beneficial metabolic effects in diabetic and Insulin-Resistant states. Diabetes, 55(8), 2256–2264. https://doi.org/10.2337/db06-0006

Utami, A. R., Maksum, I. P., & Deawati, Y. (2023). Berberine and its study as an antidiabetic compound. Biology, 12(7), 973. https://doi.org/10.3390/biology12070973

www.ingramcontent.com/pod-product-compliance
Lightning Source LLC
LaVergne TN
LVHW012033060526
838201LV00061B/4583